THE BIG TURKEY

COLORING BOOK

Flyer.Prod

FLYERPRODCO (RPROD PRESS PUBLISHING)

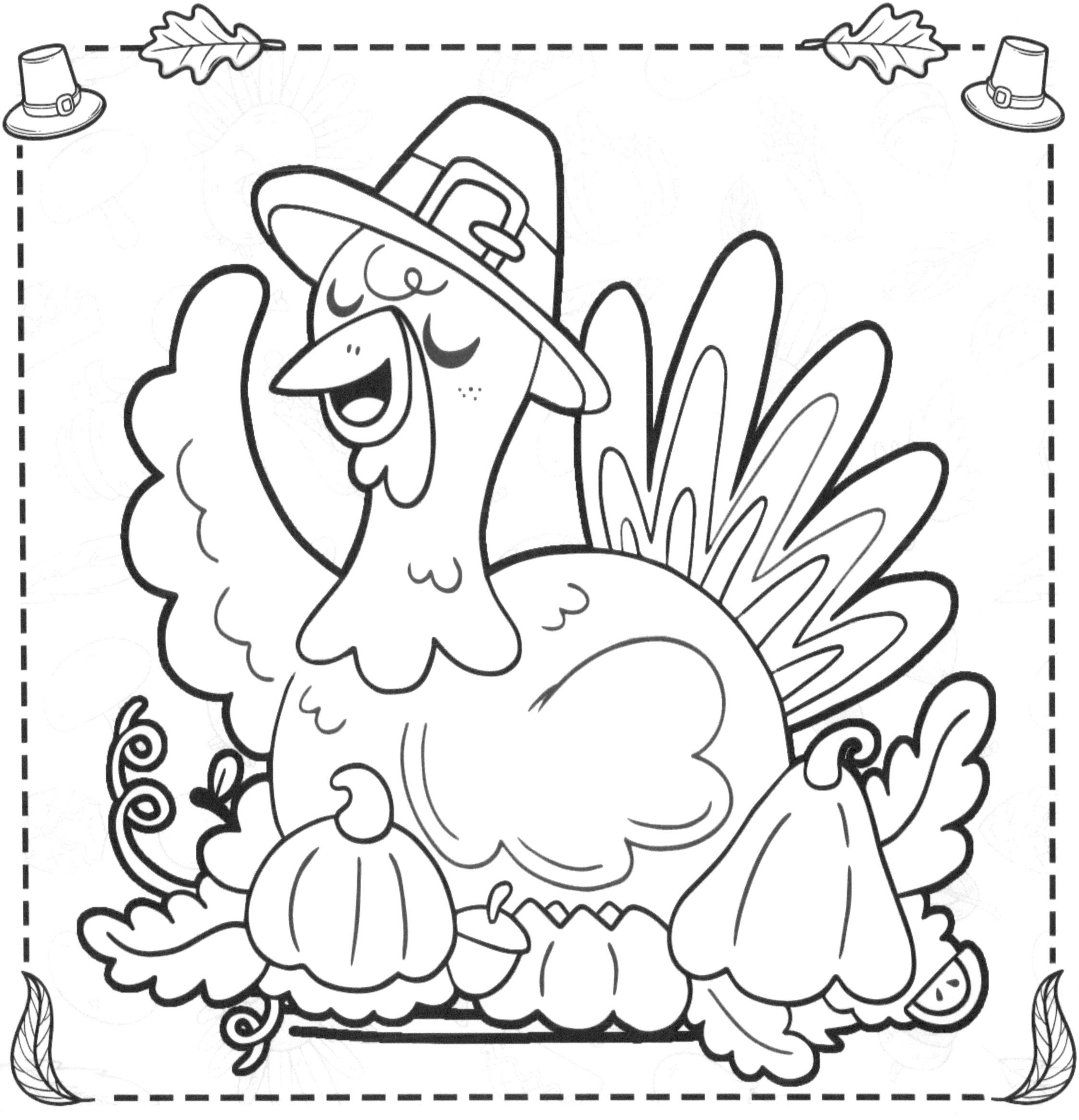

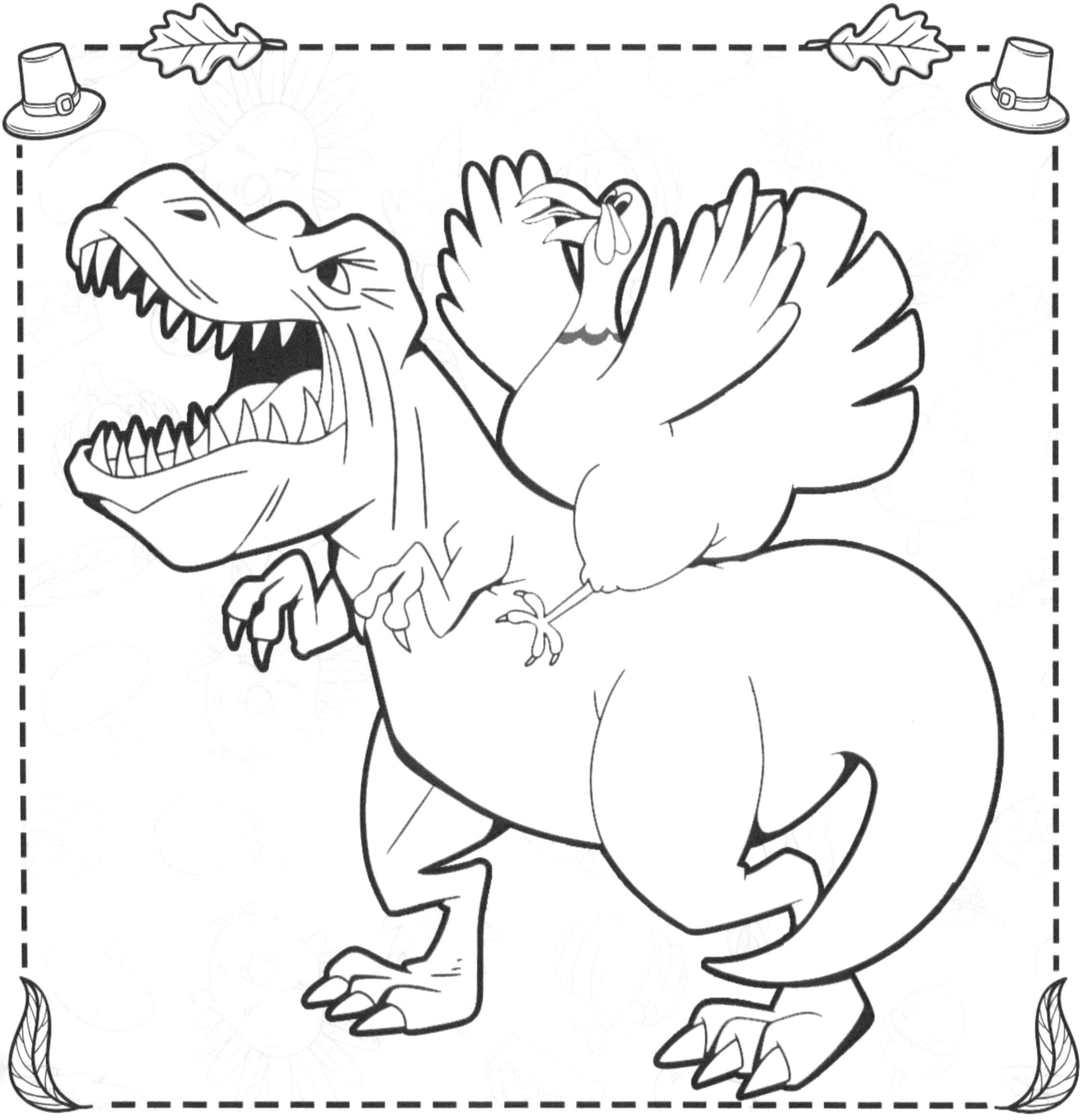

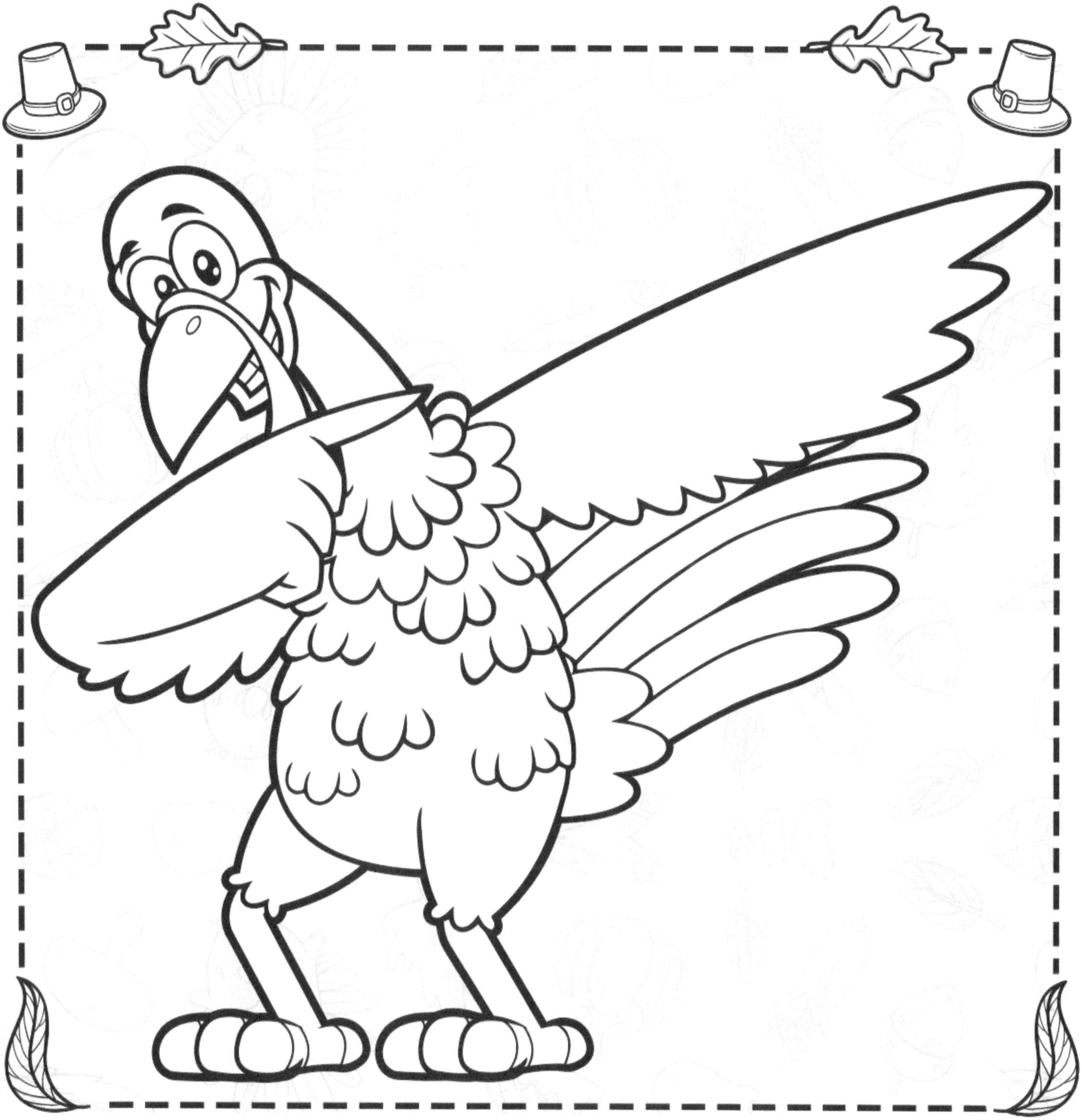

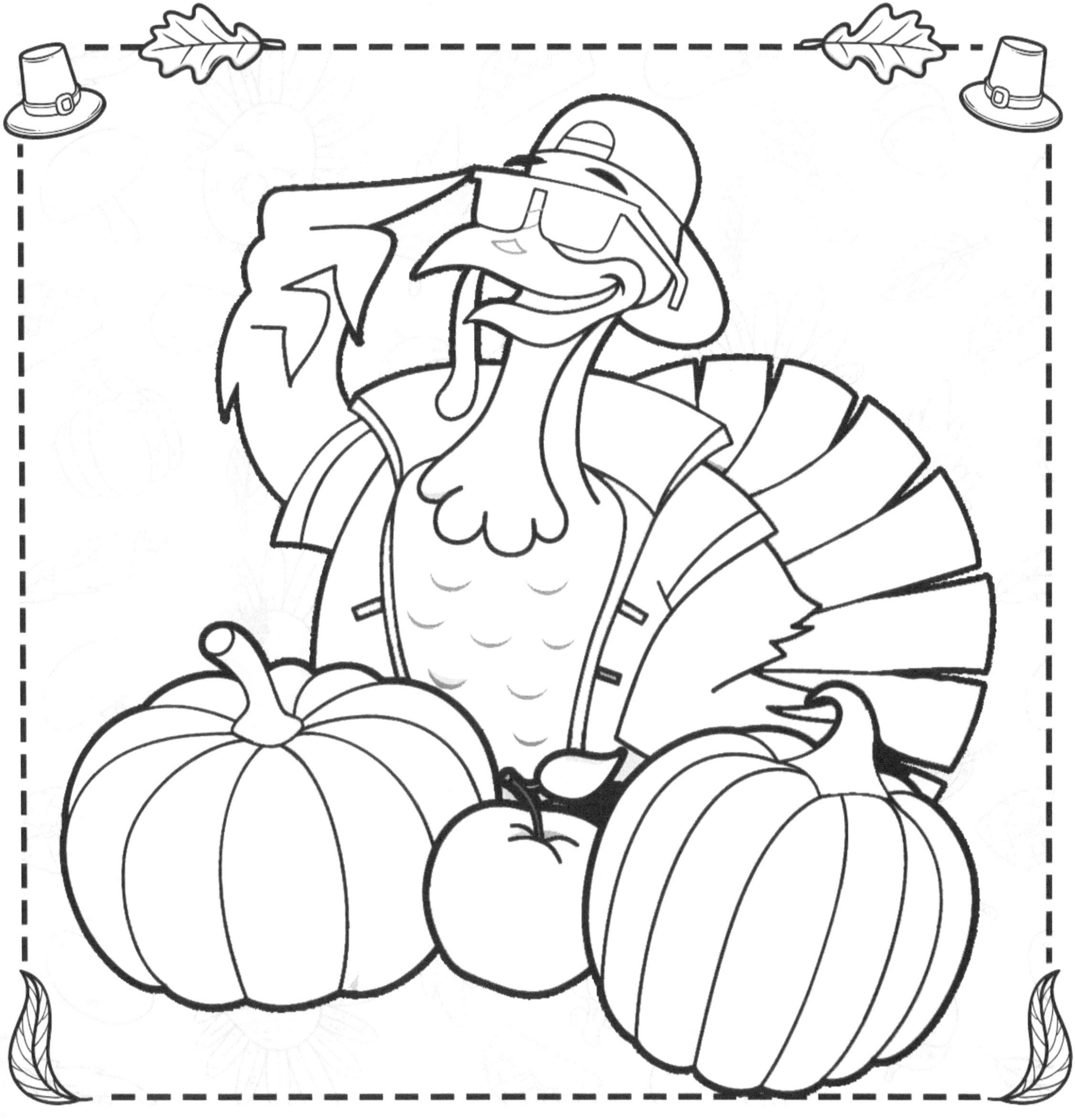

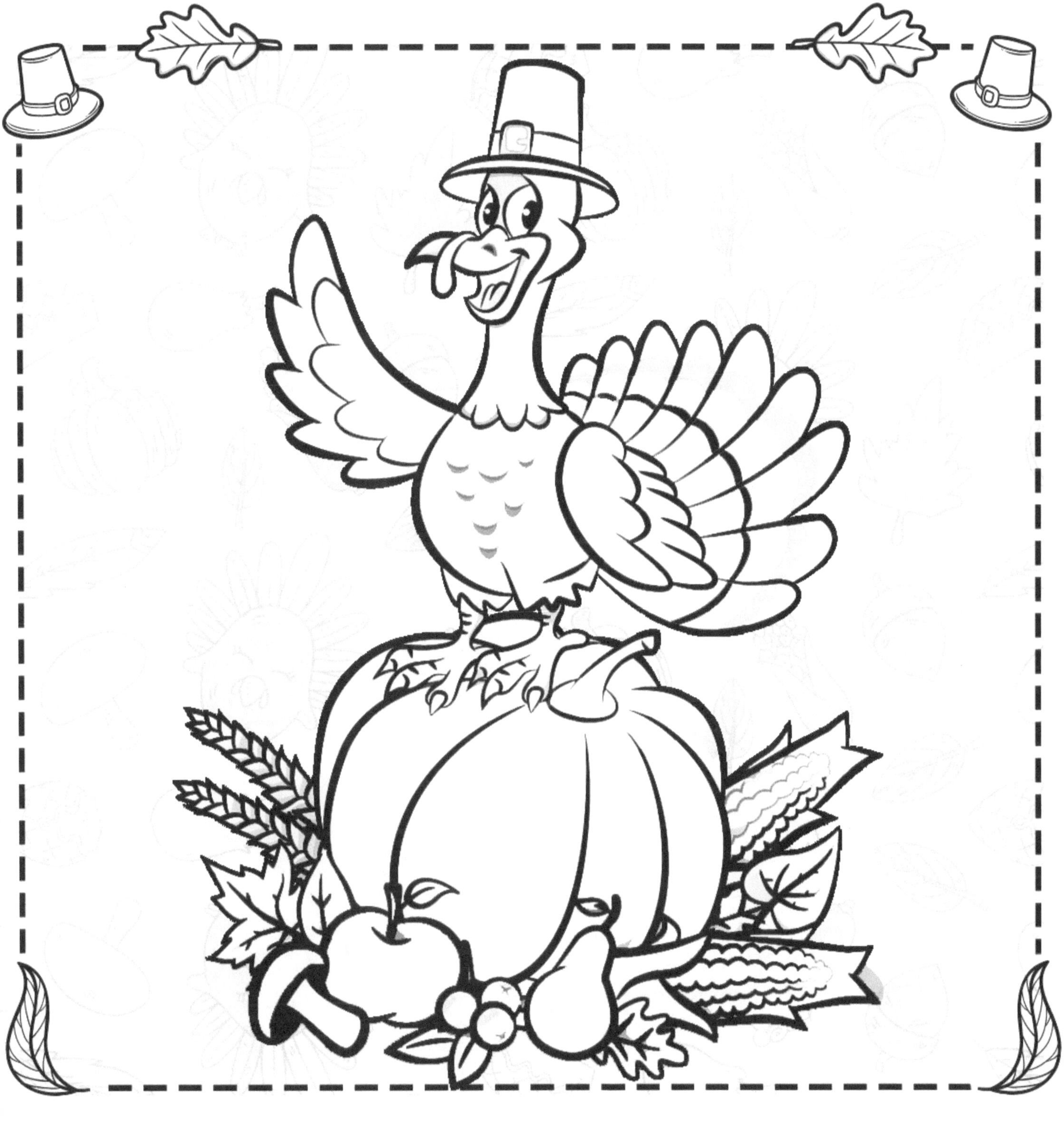

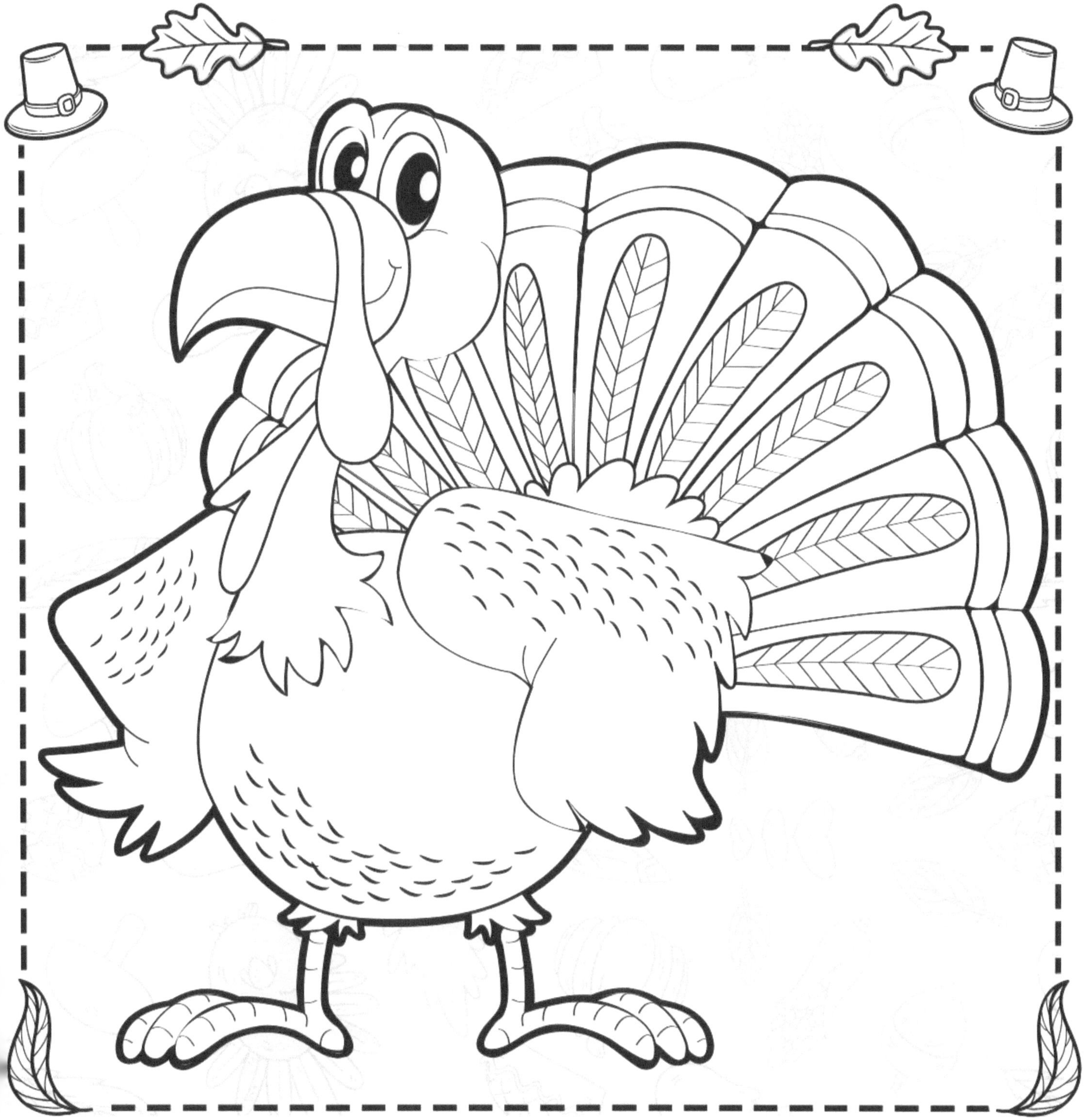

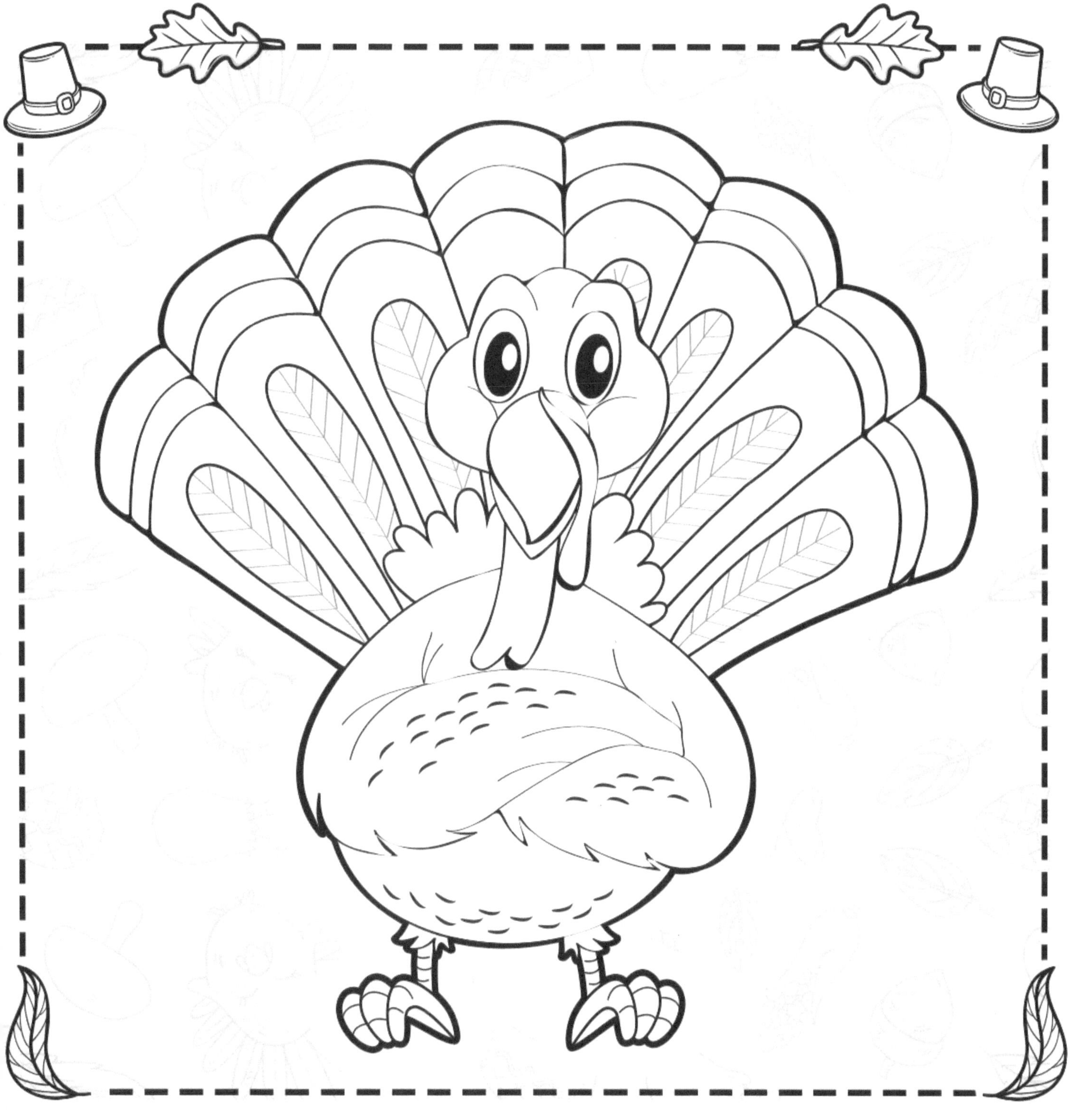

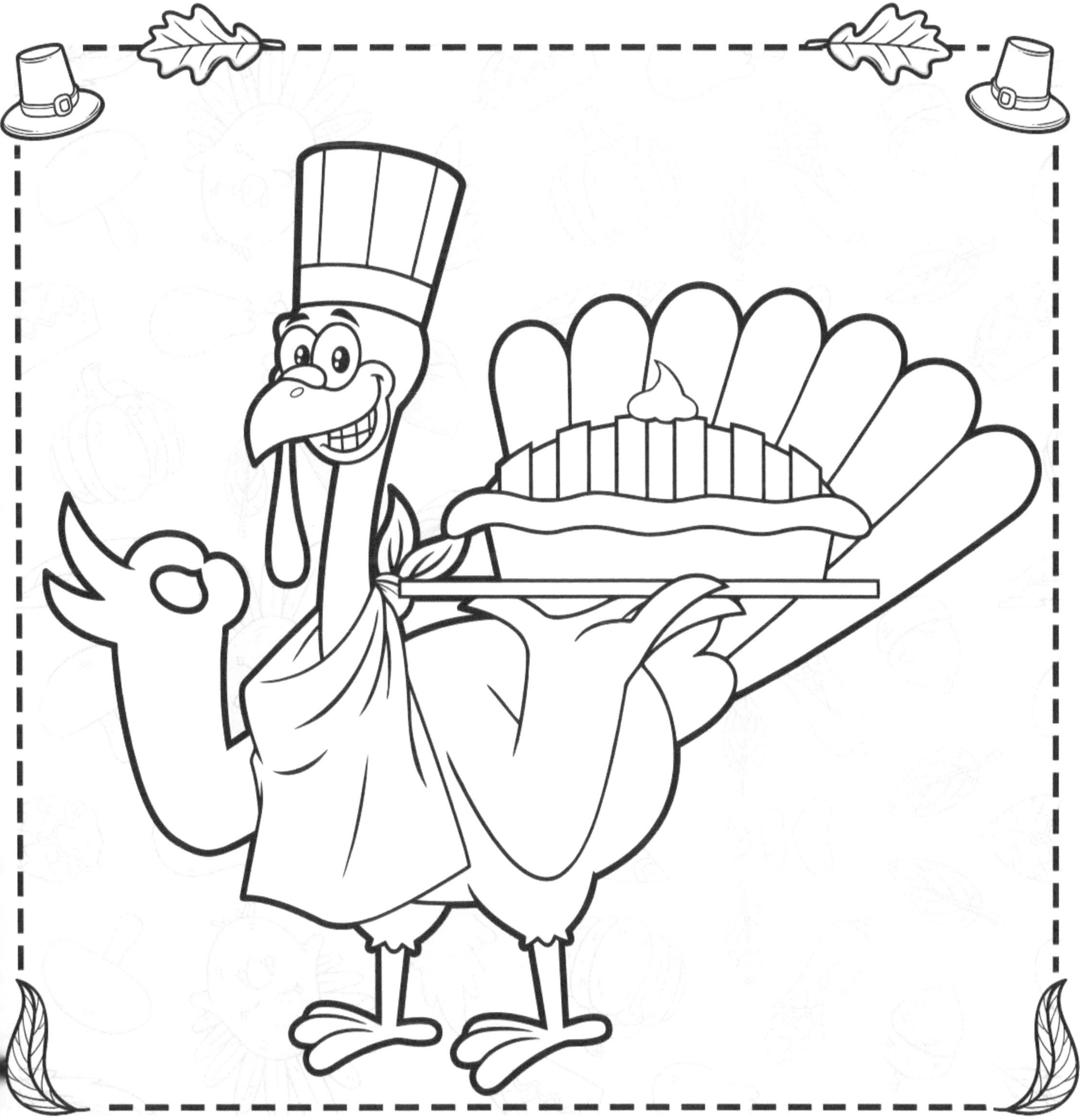

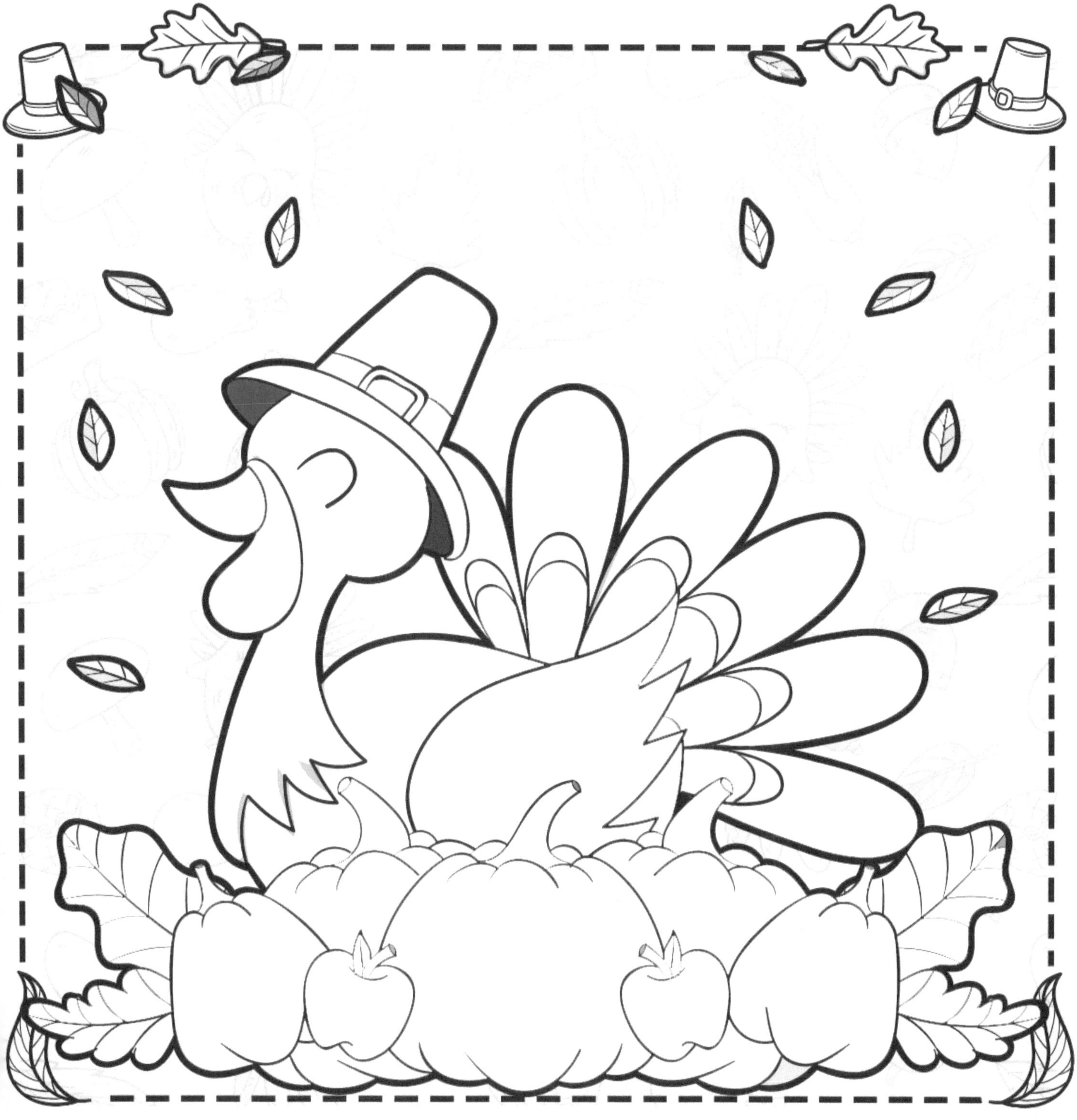

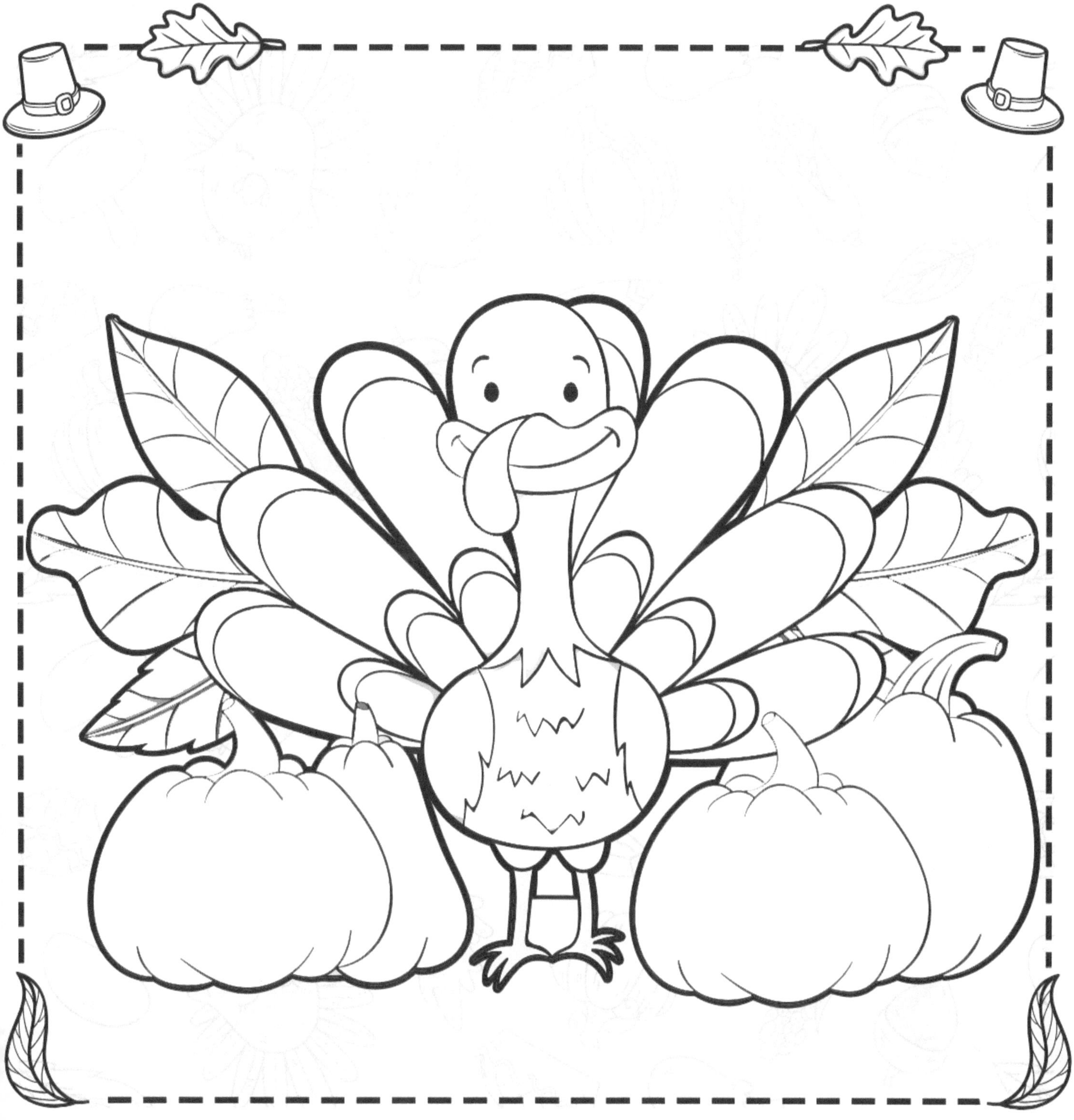

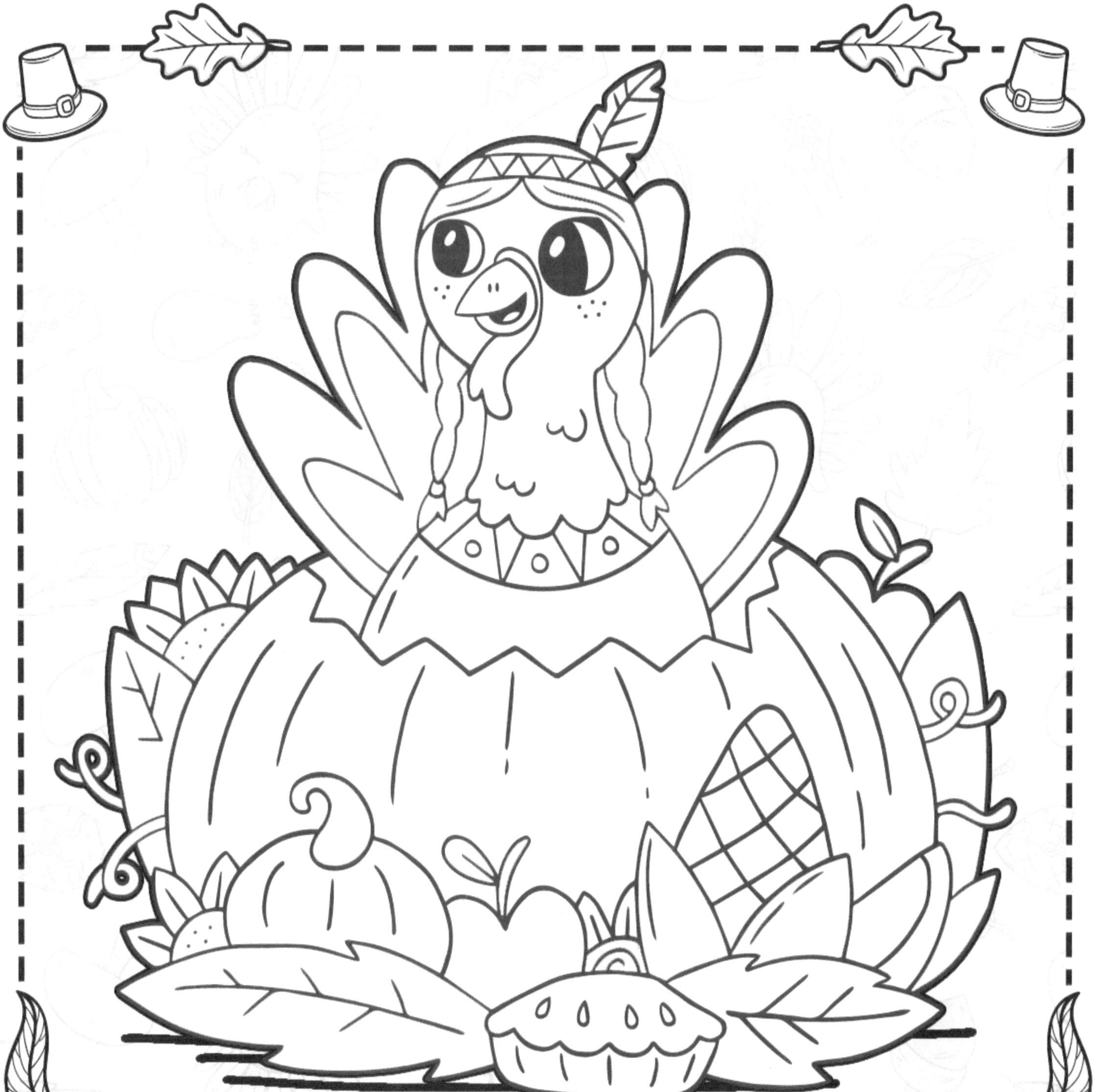

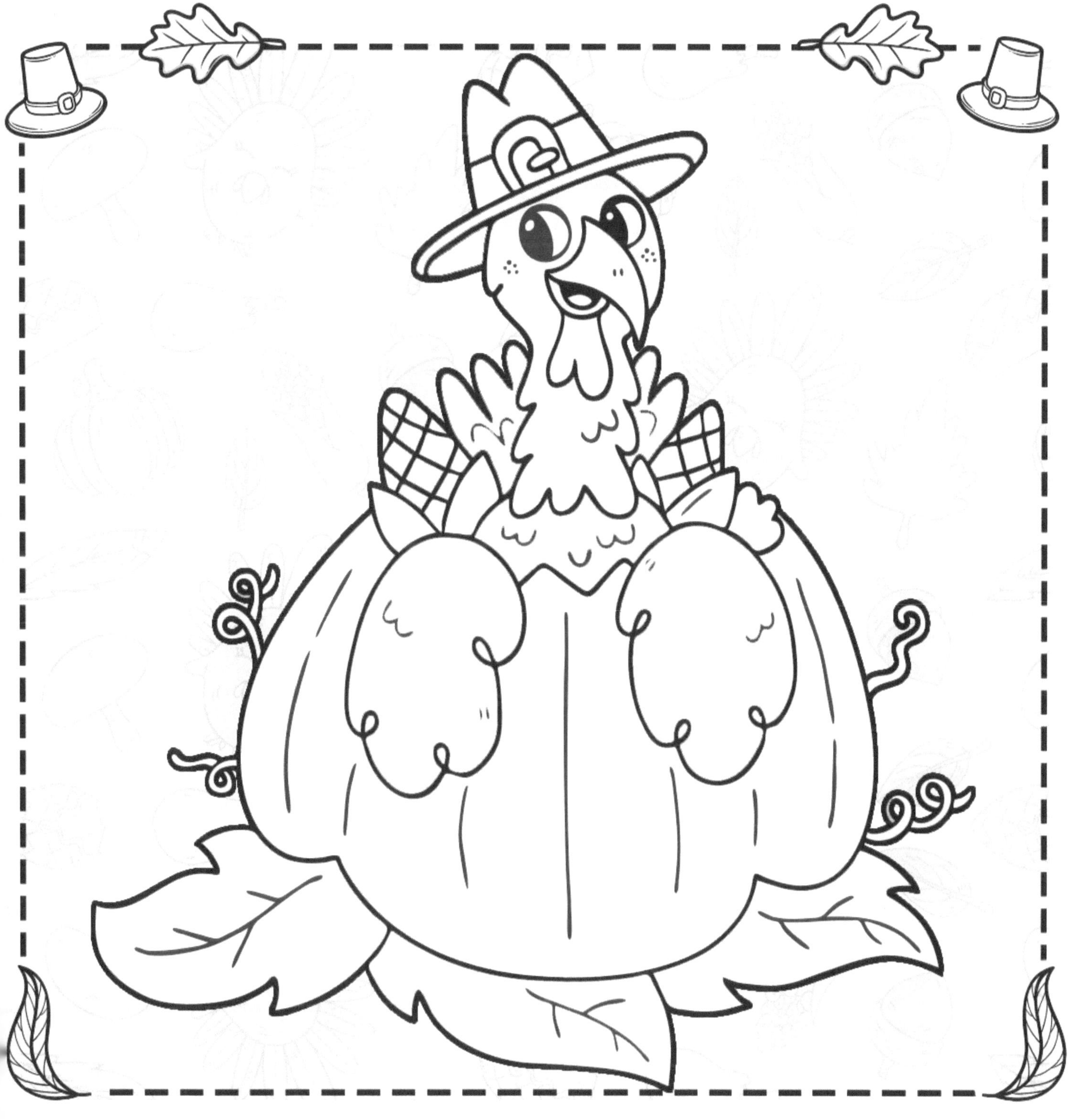

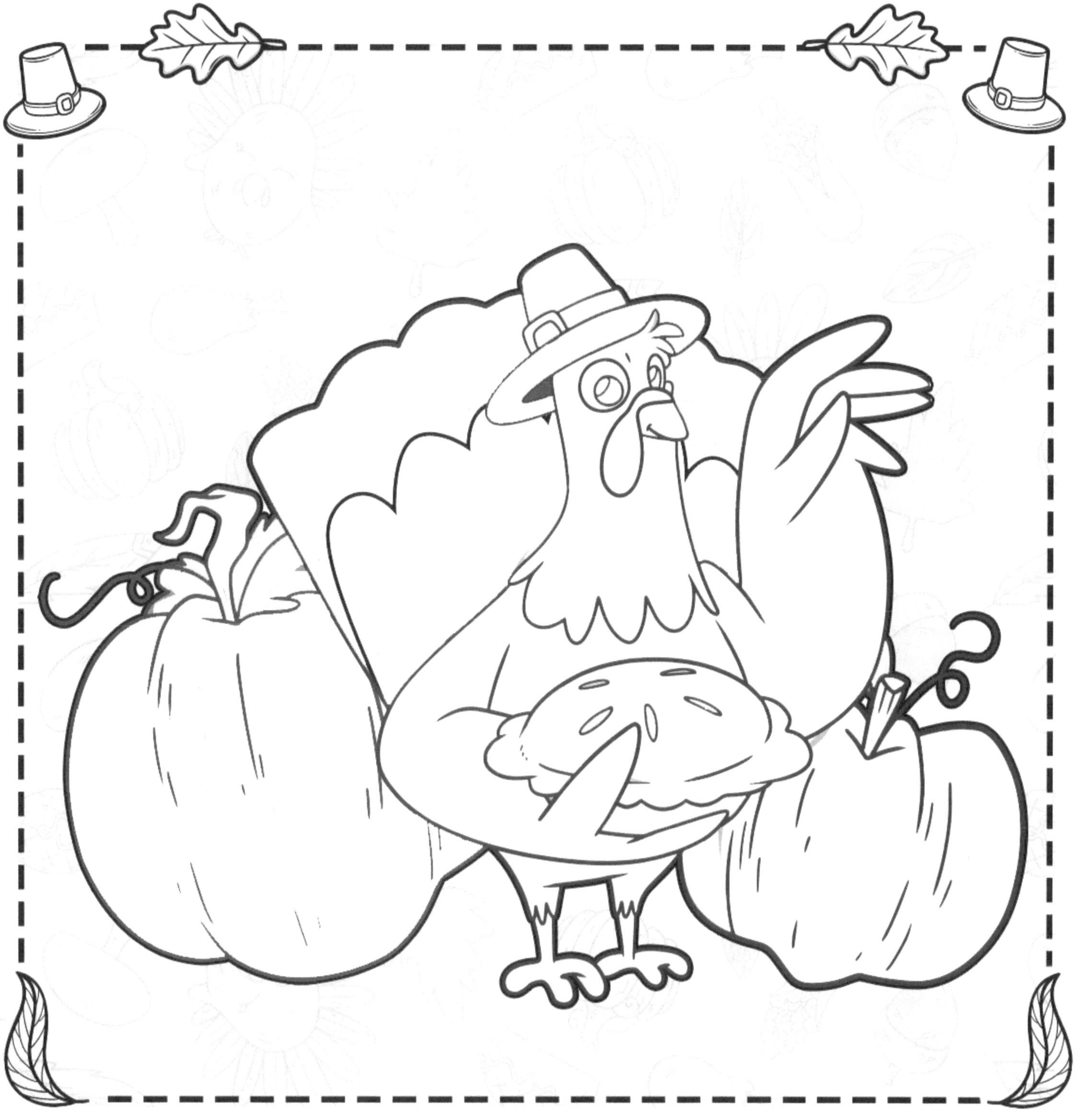

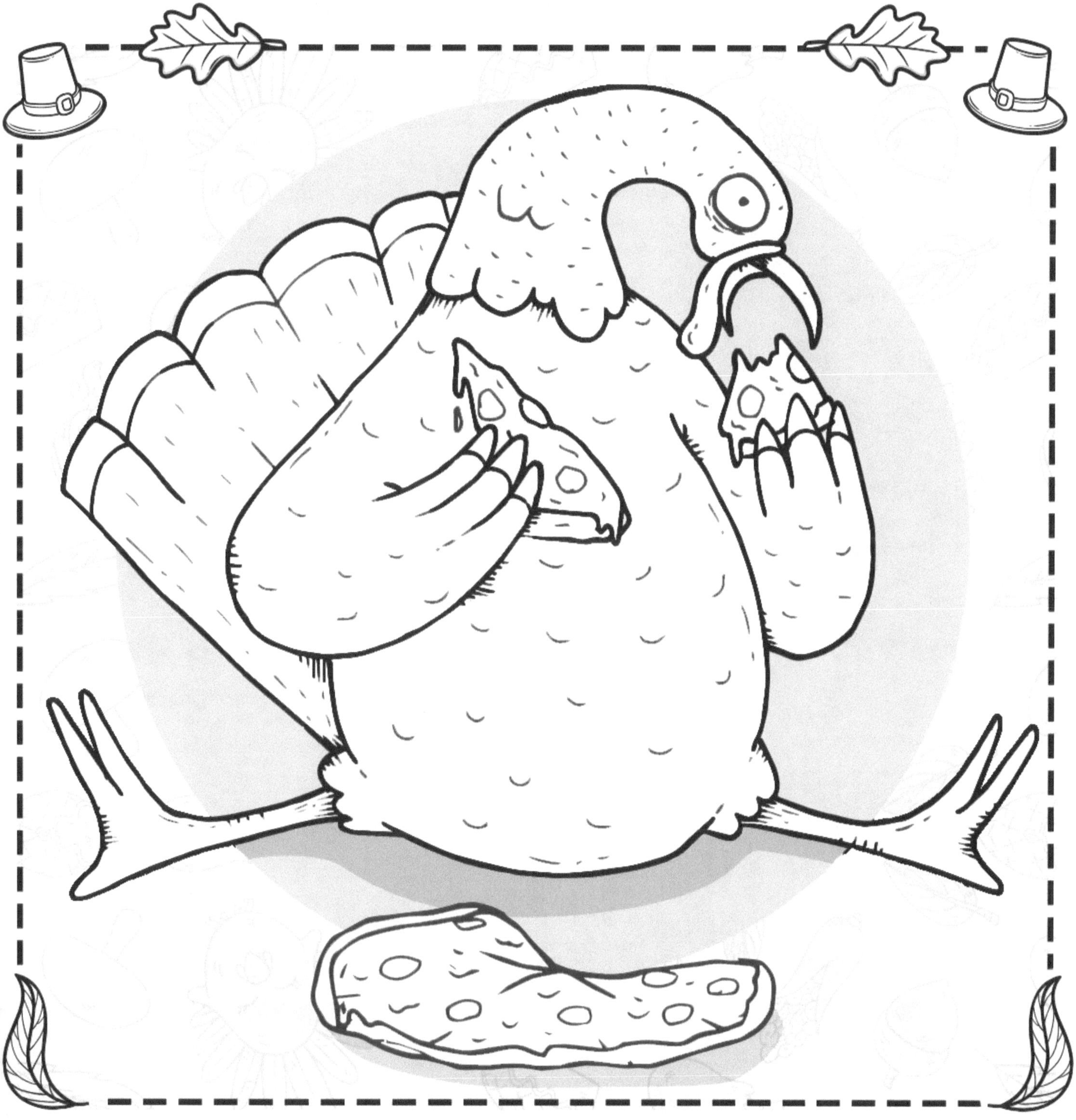

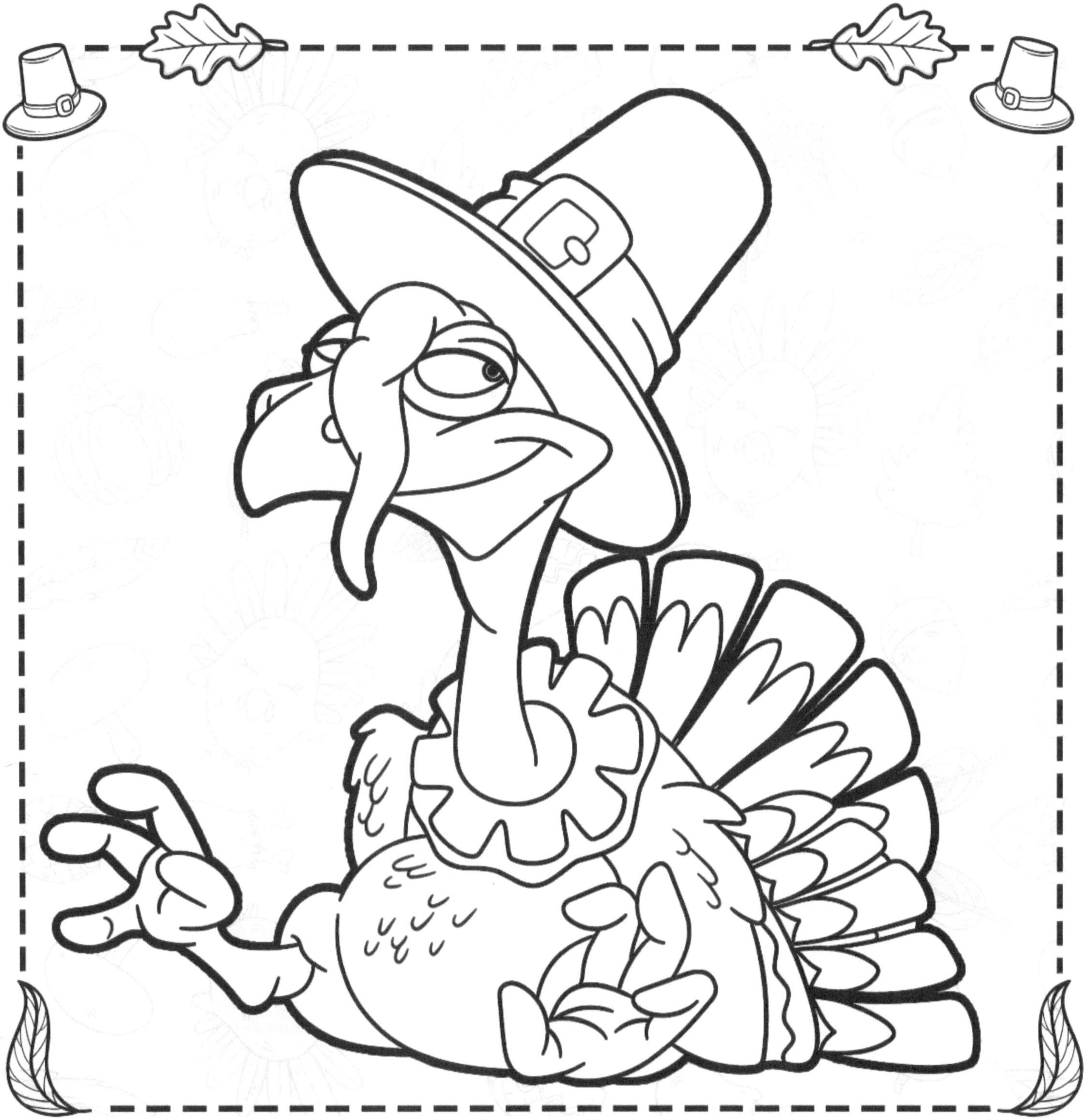

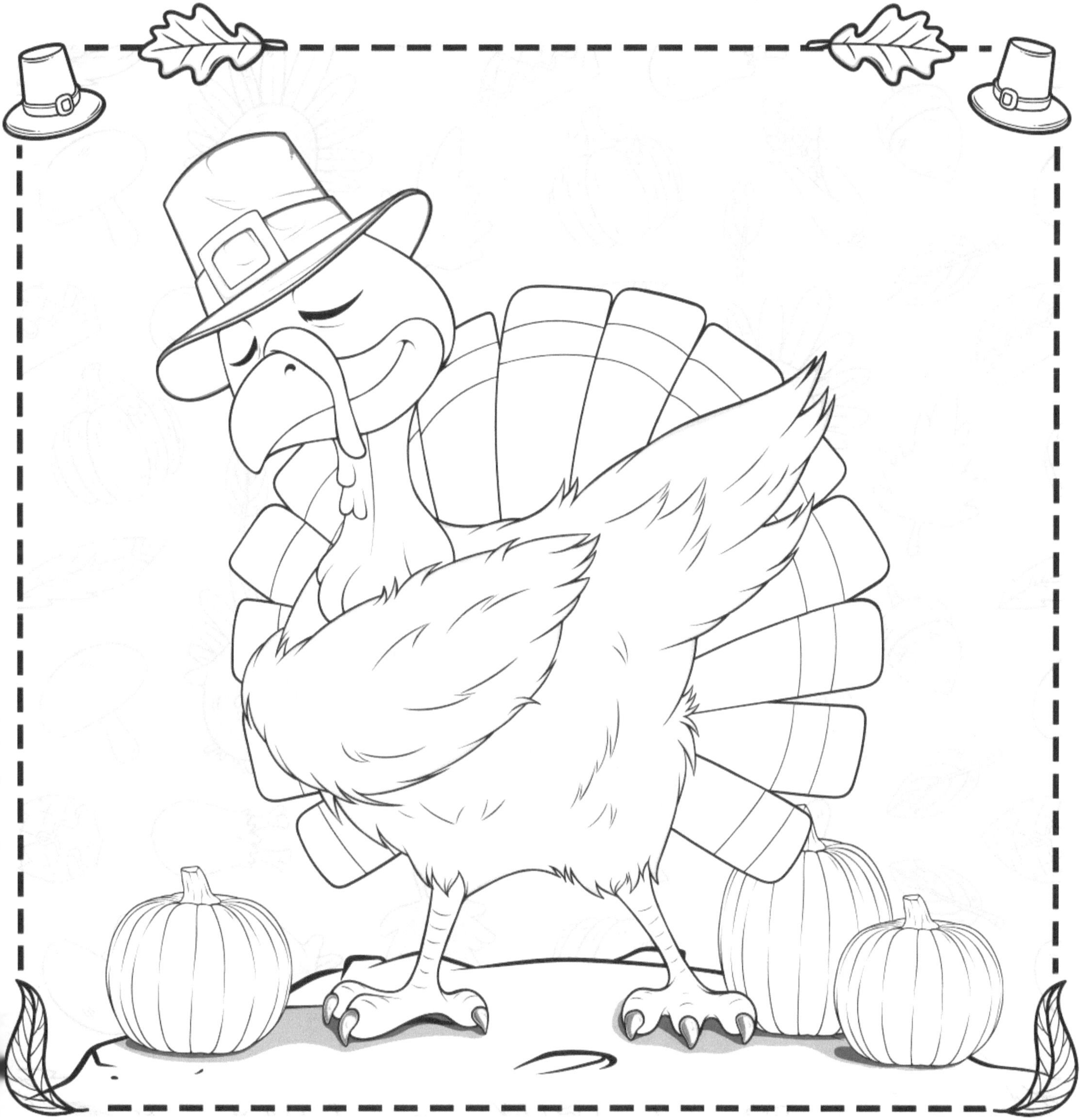

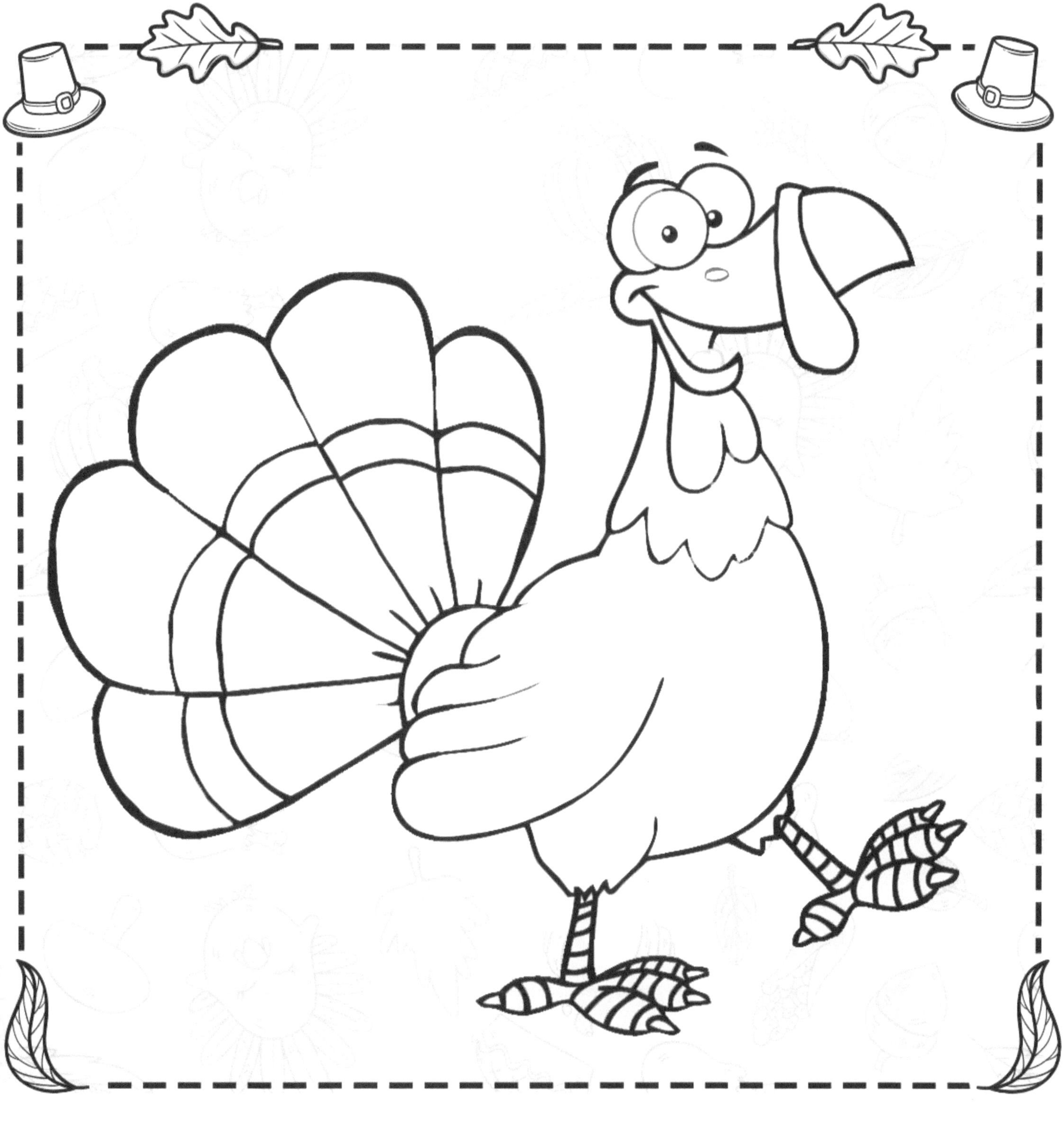

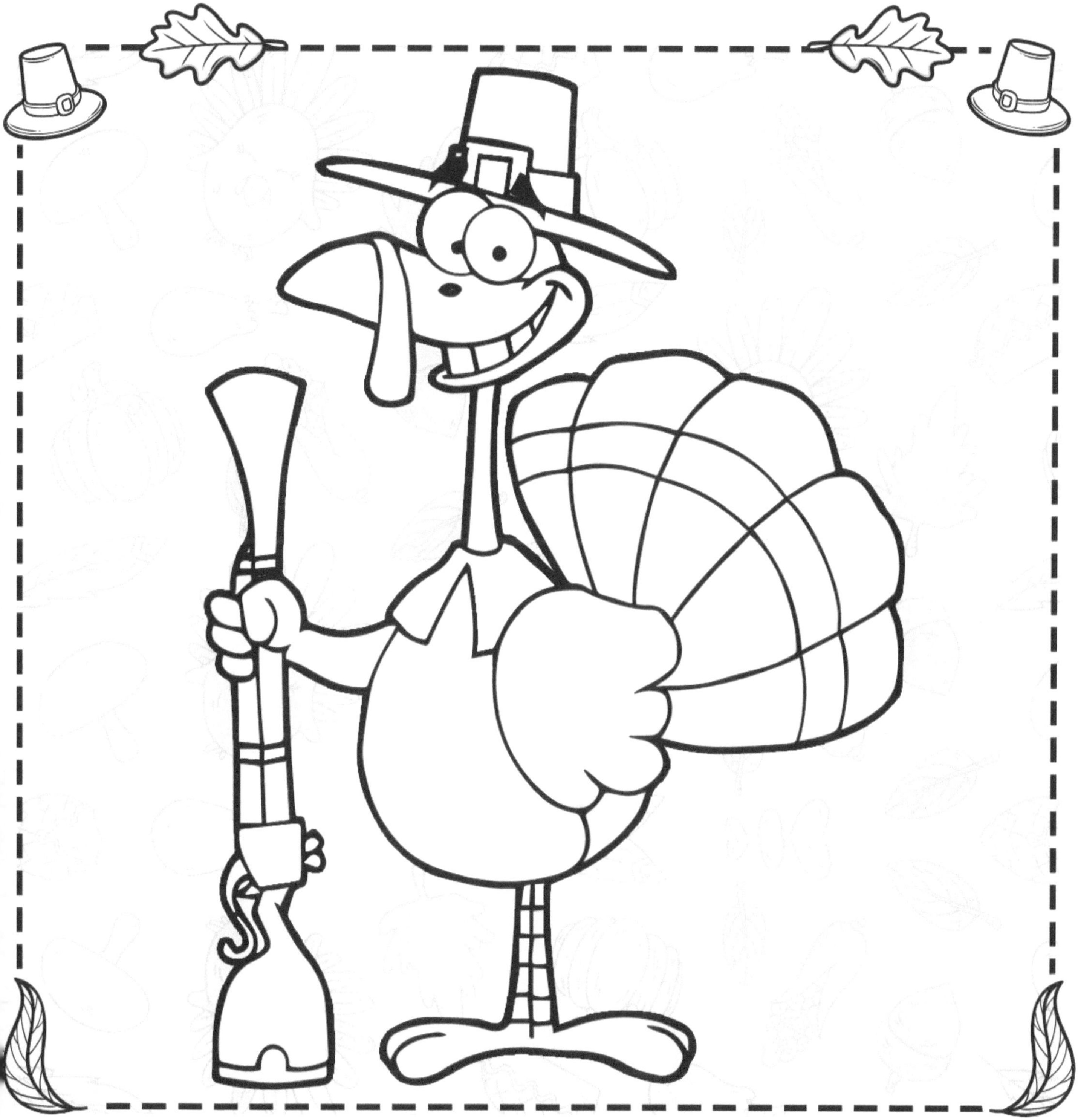

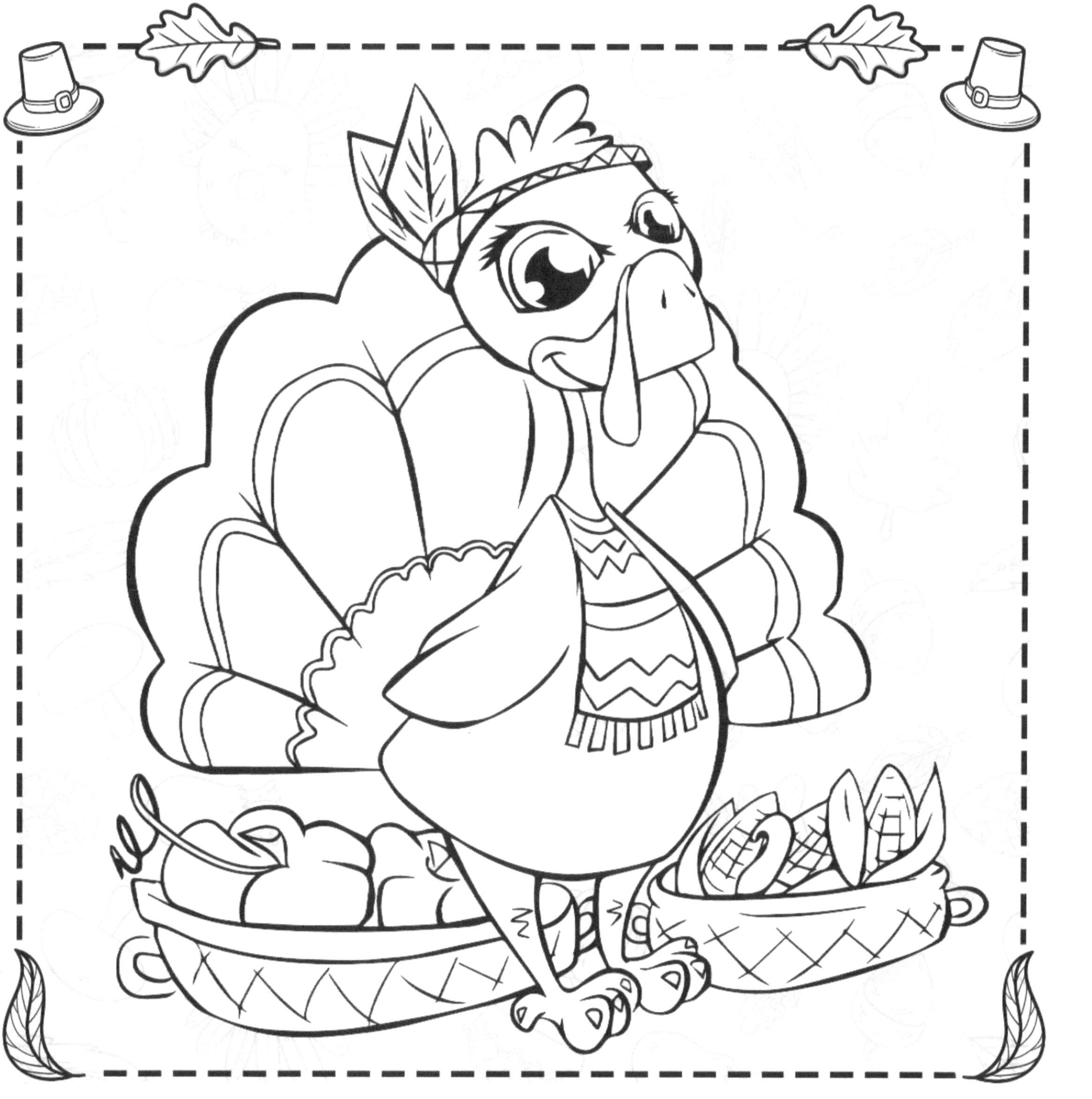

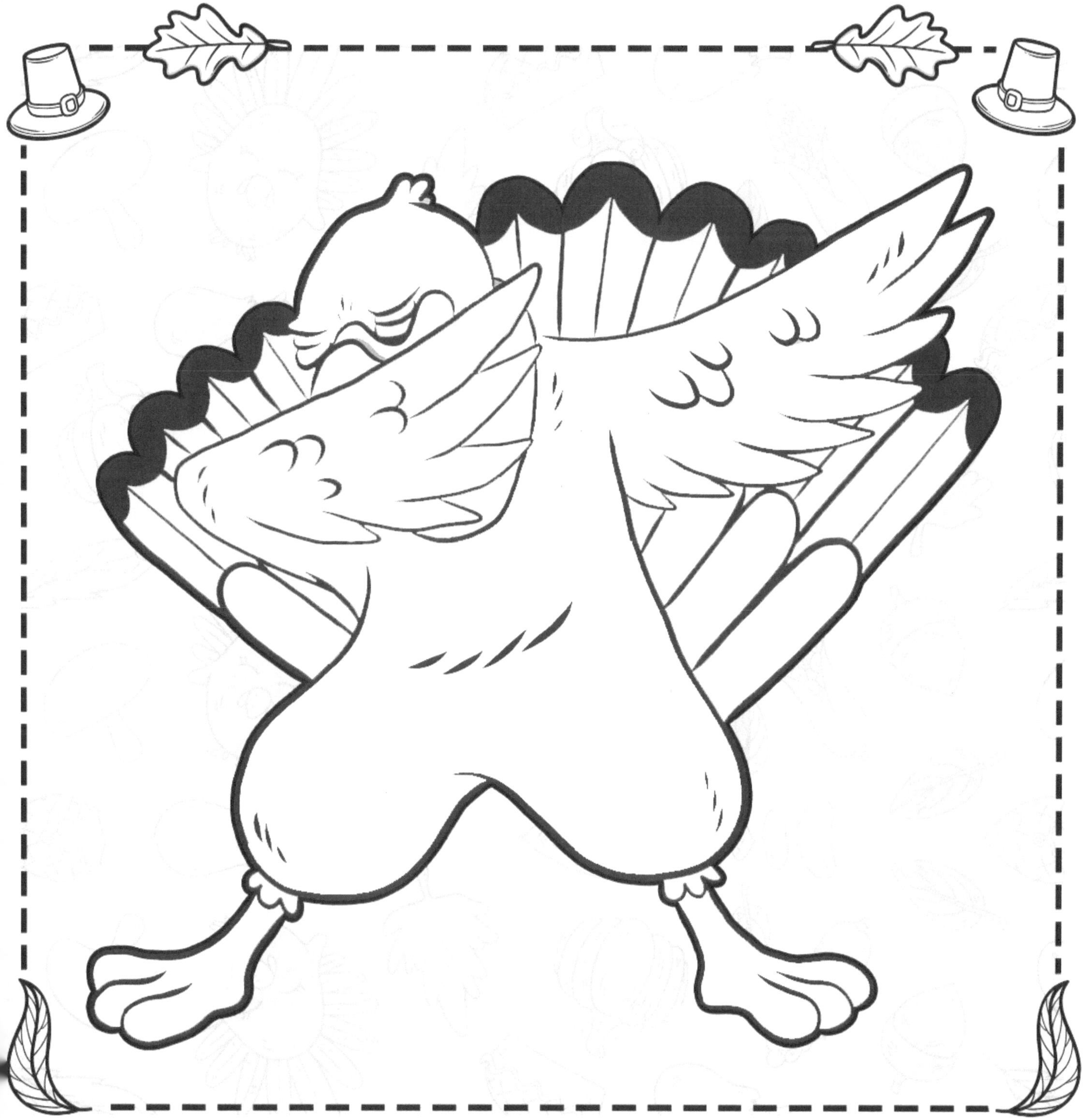

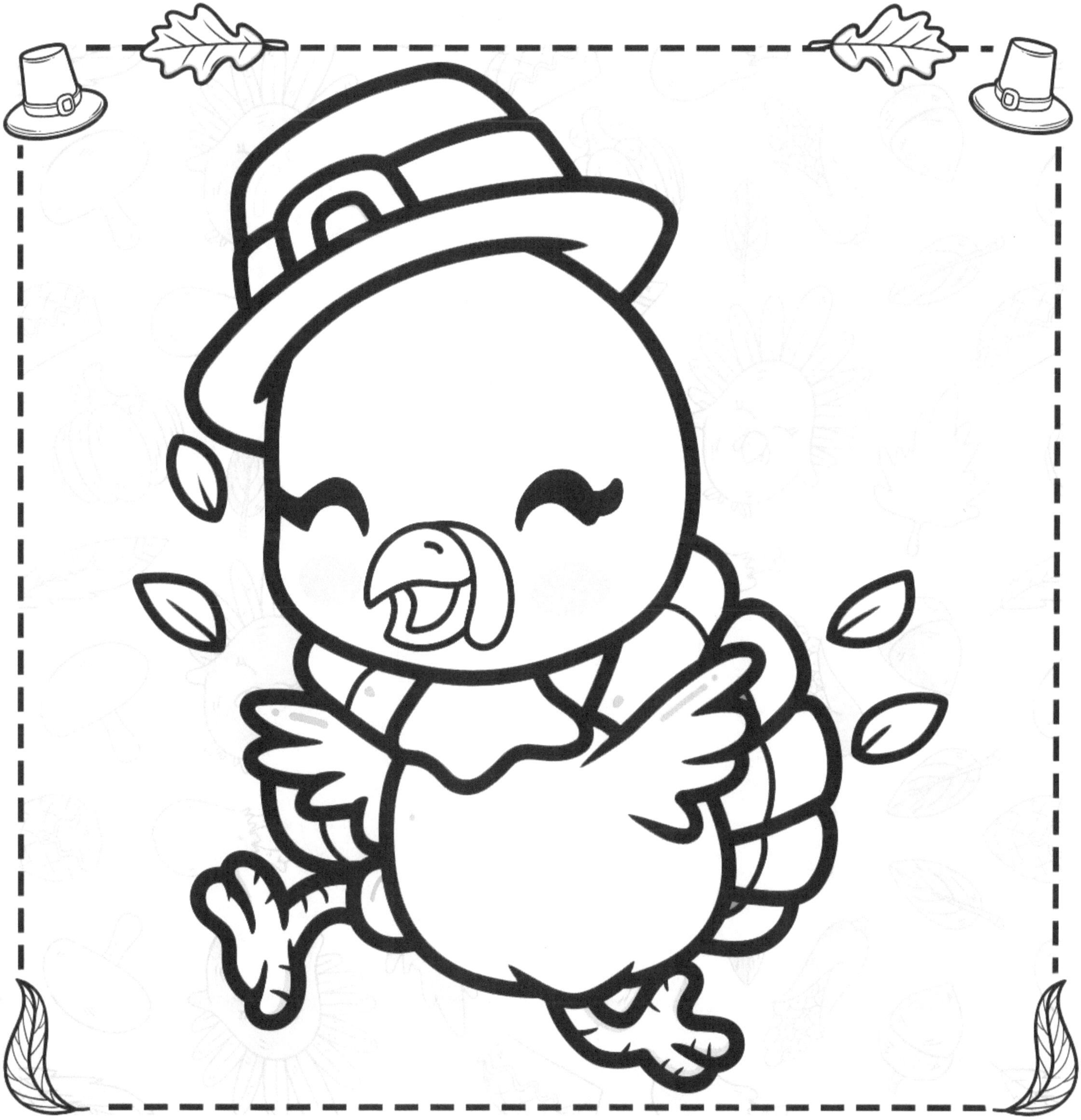

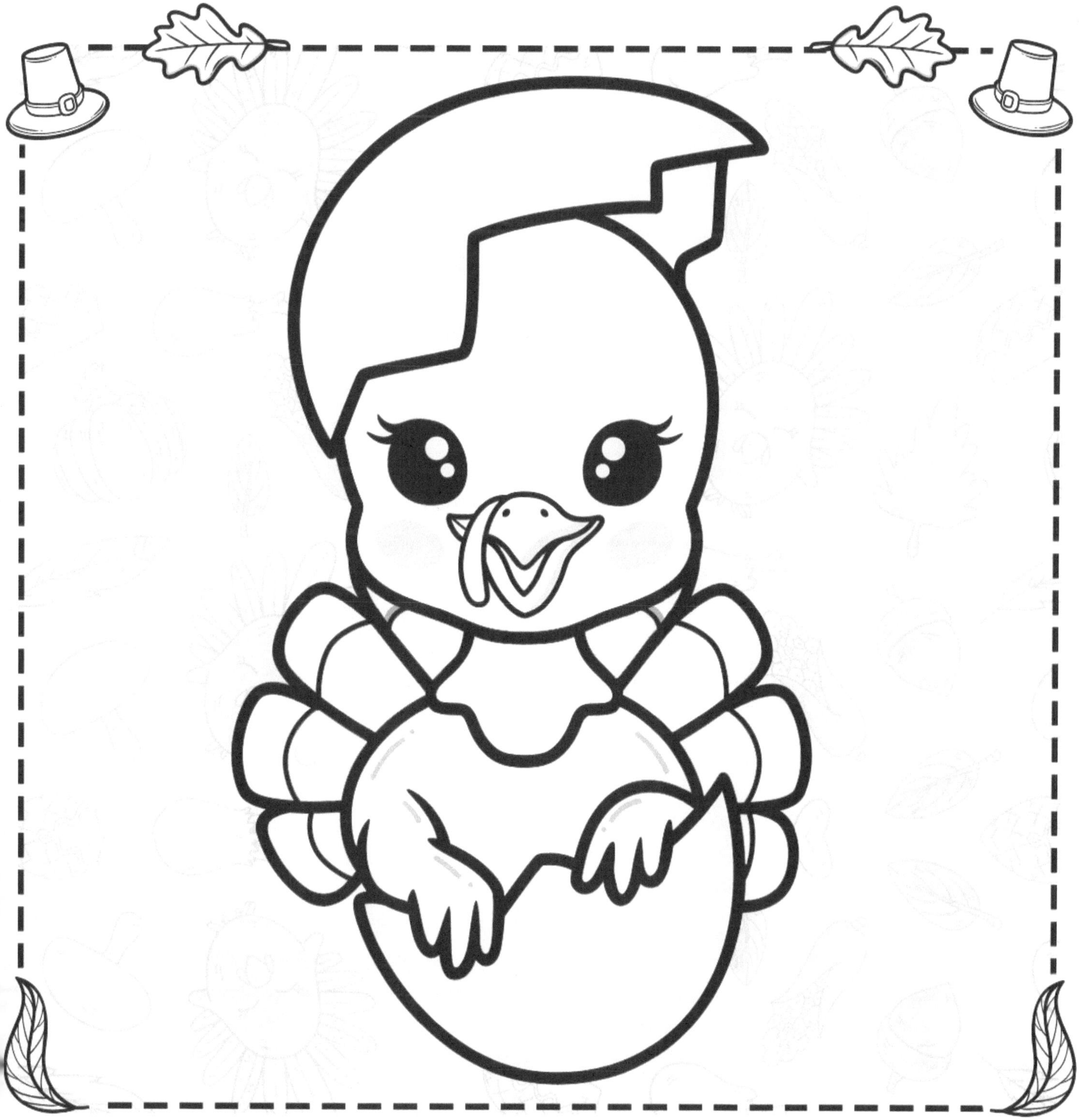

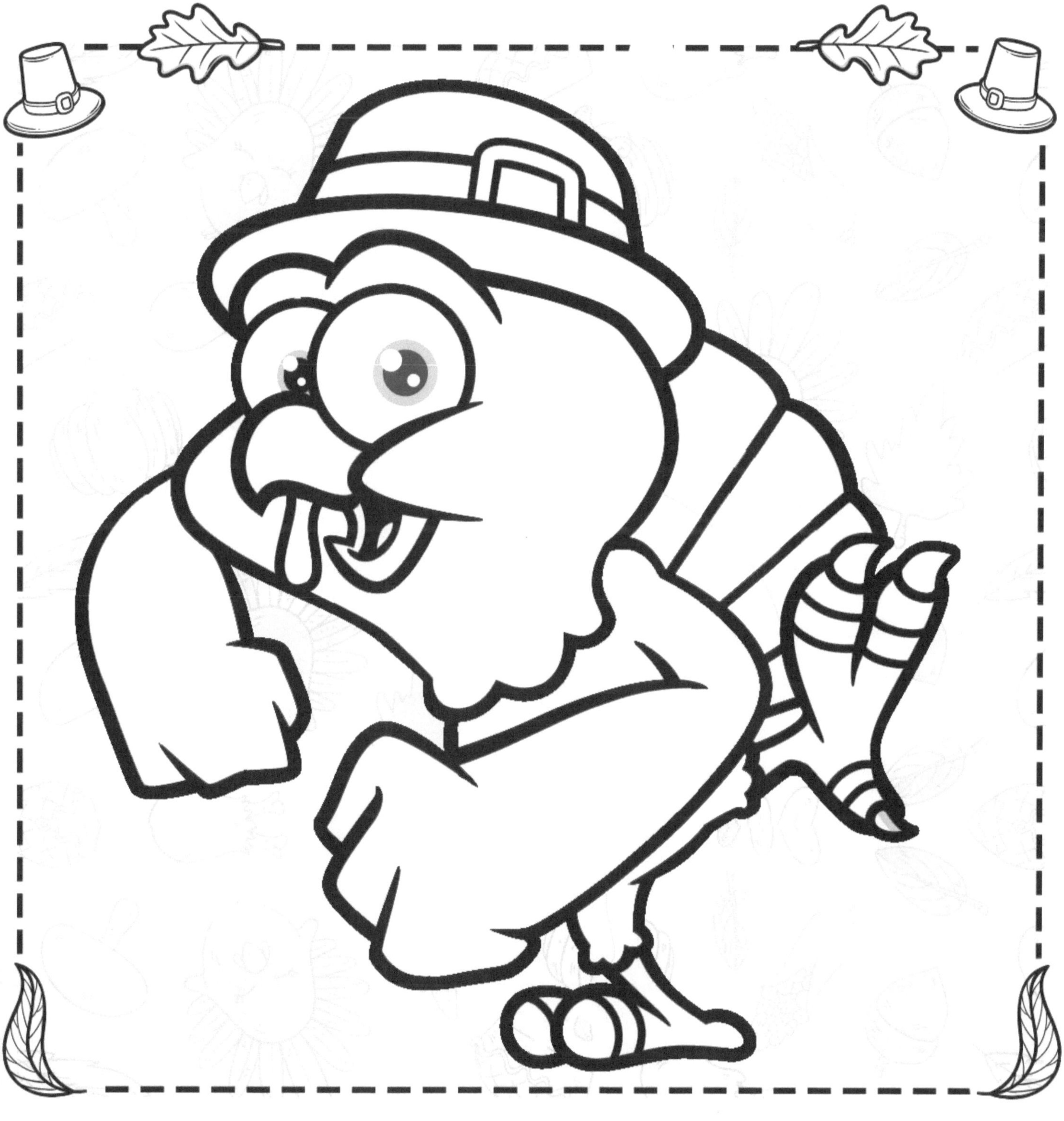

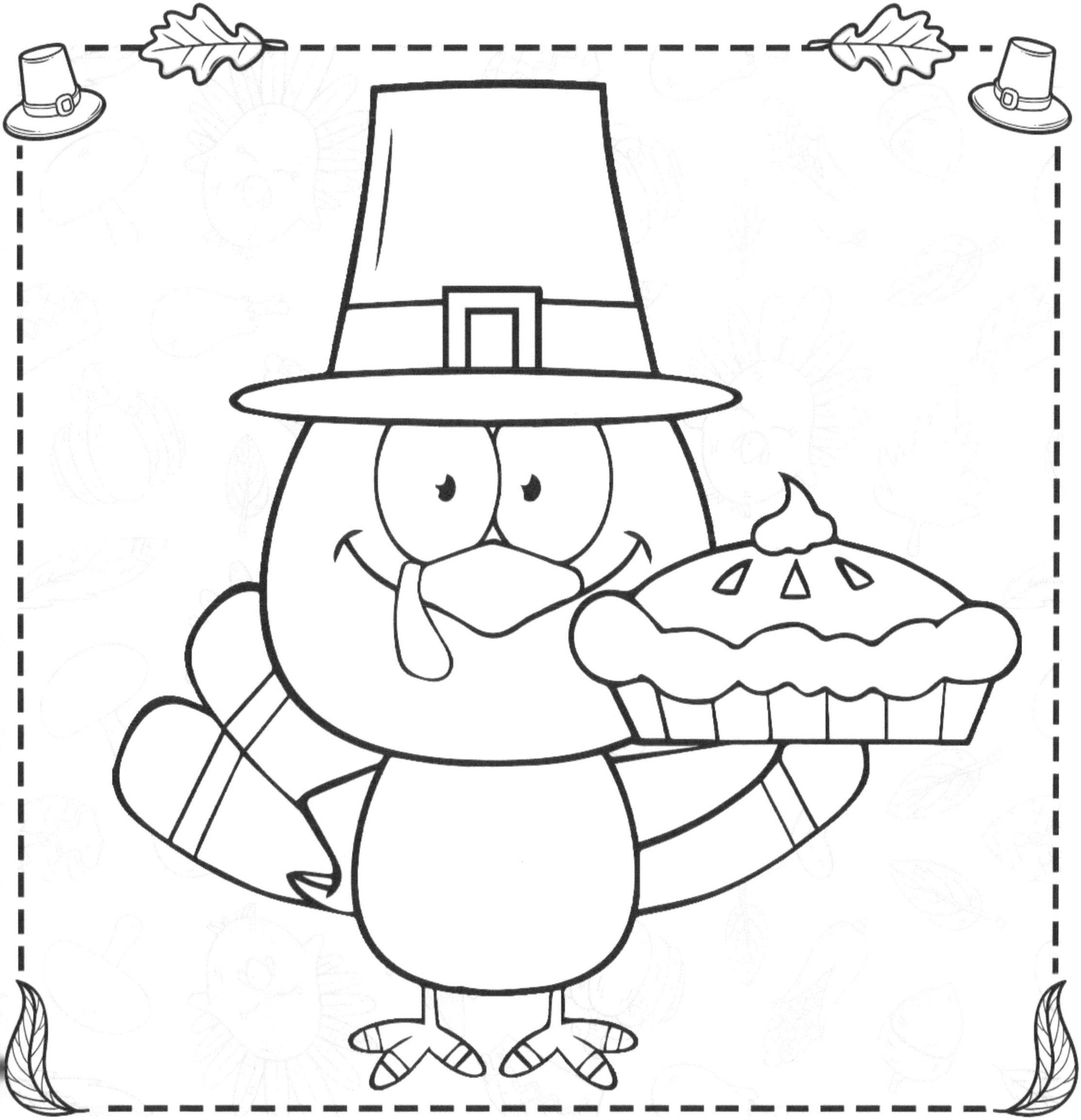

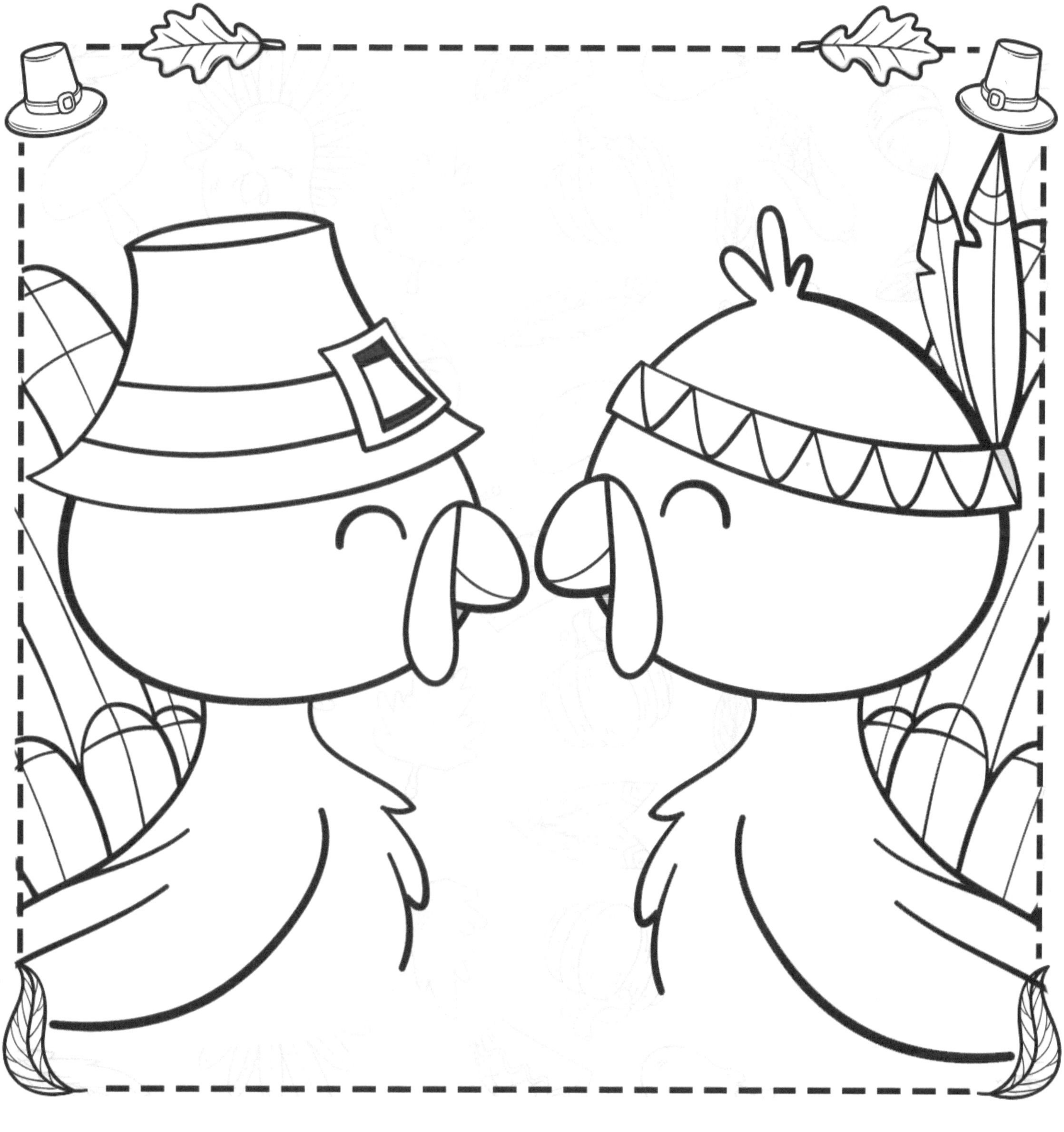

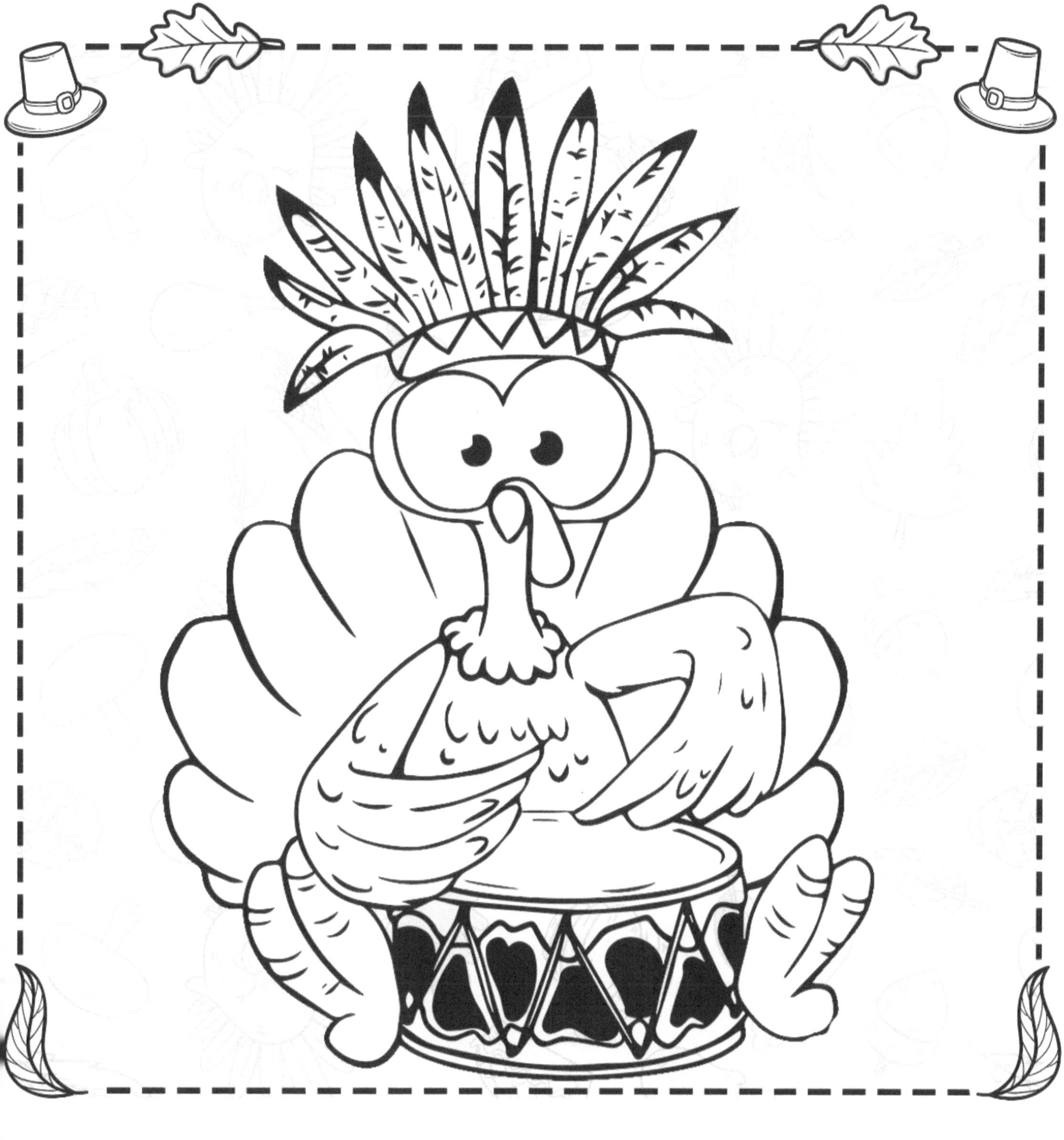

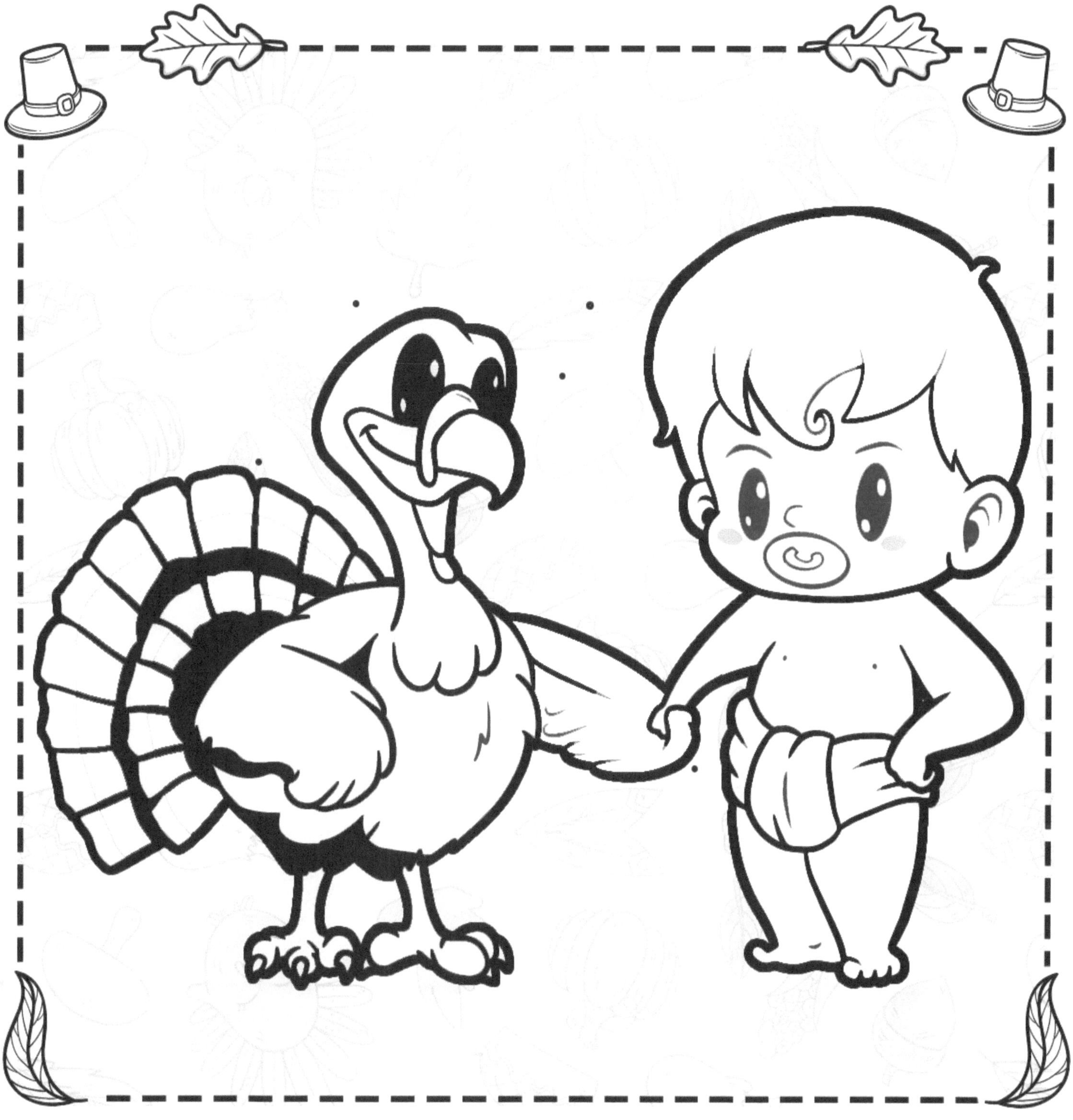

HAPPY THANKSGIVING

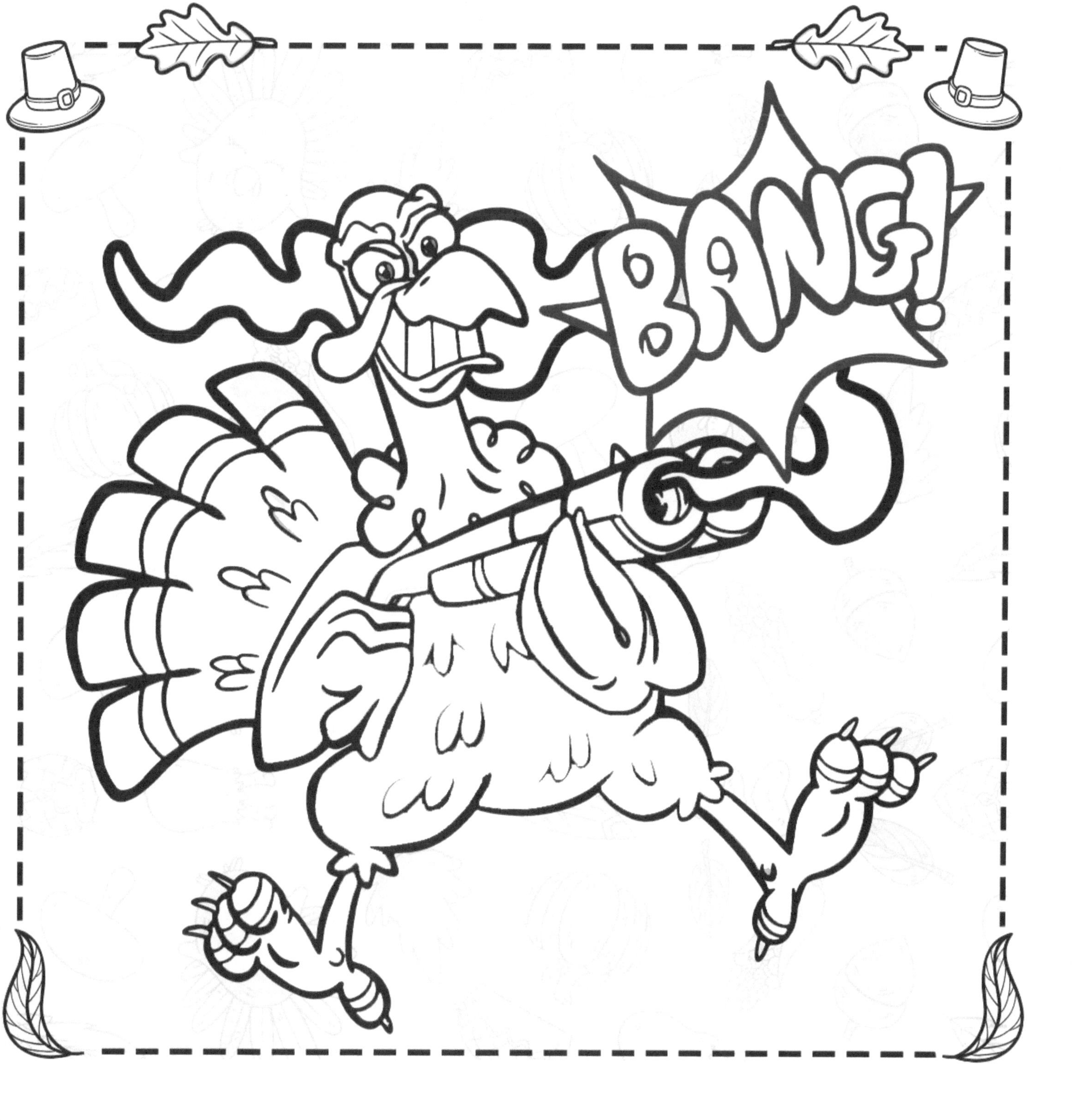
BANG!

MORE THANKSGIVING BOOKS FOR KIDS BY RPROD PRESS PUBLISHING

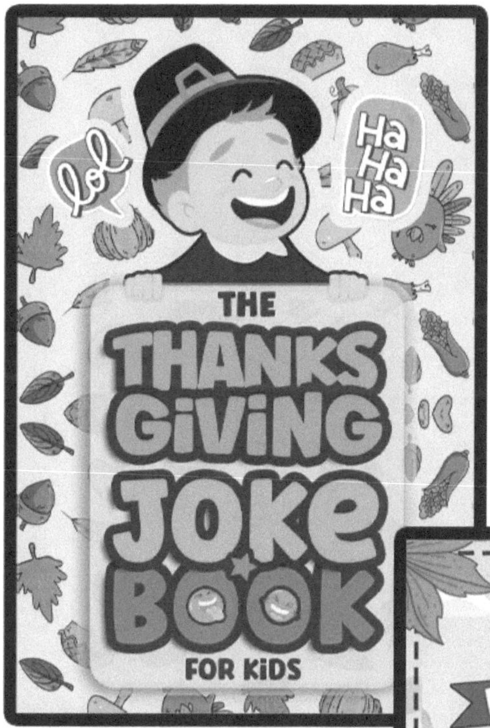

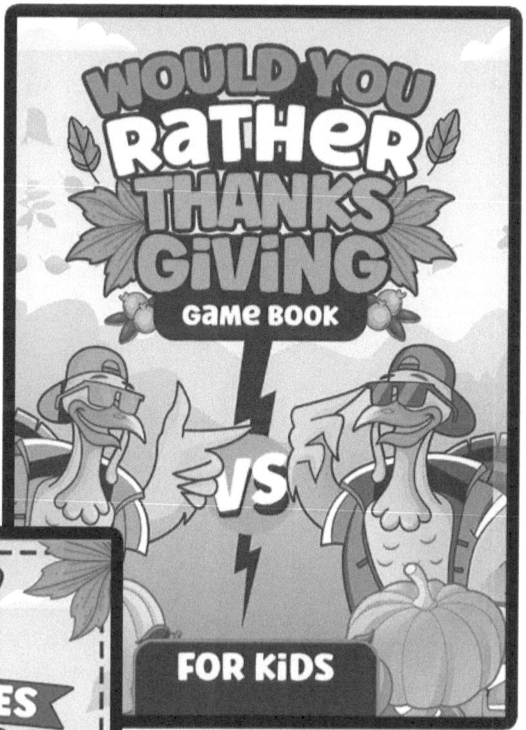

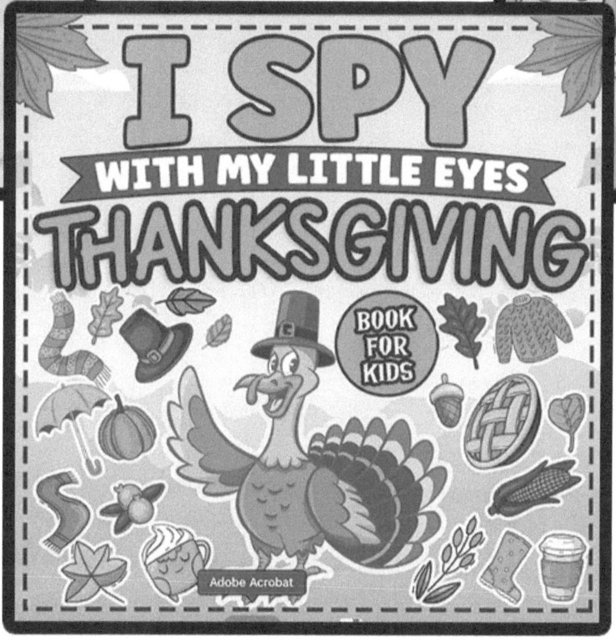

Made in United States
Troutdale, OR
11/12/2024

24728303R00038